Still Singing in the Shadows

Evelyn Nelson

Published by Evelyn Nelson, 2026.

STILL SINGING IN THE SHADOWS

First edition. February 26, 2026.

ISBN: 979-8992325348

Written by Evelyn Nelson.

FOREWORD

Is this just another book about a woman living in the shadow of her past? No! This book is unique because it focuses not solely on Silver Streak Lady but also on others singing in the shadows of their past lives. This book doesn't just address the state of the mind but, more importantly, the state of the heart.

Where can we find the one who truly understands the deep longing of our hearts? We often grow up believing that the inconsolable ache in our hearts is for a man, our mother, father, family, or material things. But no—these narratives we hold onto, thinking they will satisfy our hearts' deepest longing, fall short. The only one who can truly satisfy that longing is the ultimate Bridegroom, Christ Jesus.

Even through the darkest times in her life, Silver Streak Lady continues to sing. She diligently uses her days trusting God with unwavering faith, demonstrates virtue in her daily life, loves God with undistracted devotion, stands for physical and emotional purity, lives securely, responds to life with contentment, makes choices based on conviction, and waits patiently for God to meet her needs.

"Do not be afraid; you will not suffer shame. "Do not fear disgrace; you will forget the shame of your youth."– Isaiah 54:4 (NIV)

From a Pastor's heart, My Mom - Pastor MARY TRAMEL JOHNSON

Silver Streak Lady's first book, "Singing in the Shadows," is the untold story of a woman born to a later drug kingpin father, yet carrying the legacy of a renowned musician icon, cousin in her DNA. Despite being thrust into the foster care system, the silver thread of redemption never left her life, weaving through her pain and successes. Having had two murdered parents and experienced domestic violence, homelessness, and a near-death encounter, her resilience shines. Join us as we unravel this journey, where music, divine connections, and unwavering faith guide her through life's rollercoaster. Can we feel and hear God through her life—and in ours?

INTRODUCTION

The sky was heavy with clouds the day she first recognized the pattern—the silver streaks cut across her life like slivers of light breaking through thunderheads. They came unexpectedly, often in moments when shadows seemed the longest, illuminating paths she didn't know existed. This was the life of the woman they called "Silver Streak Lady," a name given not by the world but by how she chose to rise, again and again, as if woven from threads of something stronger than mere circumstance.

To outsiders, hers was a life stitched together by tragedy. The daughter of loss, a child of the forgotten, and a woman shaped by the weight of abandonment, her story might have resembled many others—except for the light that continued to surface: the silver streaks. As a child, she would watch storms roll in over the small home she temporarily called hers. In the dead of night, lightning would slice the darkness, illuminating everything for a moment—bare feet pressed against the cold floor, the shadows on the walls transforming into ghosts of memory, the faint outline of a worn teddy bear lying beside her. Those flashes were fleeting, but they revealed what existed beyond the night. In time, she understood that her life carried those same moments—blinding pain and relentless fear, yet threaded with slivers of light too persistent to ignore.

From the beginning, life seemed determined to keep her hidden, folded away in corners where no one could see. Born to a father tangled in the underworld of crime and a mother whose beauty was shadowed by violence, her path seemed predestined for hardship. By the time she was barely old enough to form memories, the weight of loss pressed down on her like a second skin.

She learned early that some people carried shadows within them. Those shadows whispered in the voices of adults who came and went from the small rooms where she and her brothers stayed. They manifested in foster homes where the walls were cold, the beds stiff, and the rules unwritten but unbreakable. Yet, even then, in the dimmest moments, she would hum—quiet melodies that rose unbidden to her lips, songs she couldn't name but felt as though they belonged to her.

It was in those melodies that the first silver streaks began to form. They were soft at first, little threads of warmth that curled around her heart when the world felt the most indifferent. Music became her language long before she found the words to explain her pain.

"Silver Streak Lady" was not a name given lightly. It was a title born from survival, from the countless times she stood on real and metaphorical stages, bearing witness to her strength. Those who met her saw not just a survivor but a woman who wore her scars like medals—proof of battles fought and won.

Each streak of silver in her story marked a moment when the world tried to break her and failed. The death of her mother was one. Her father's murder, another. Homelessness, betrayal, and near-death experiences stitched themselves into the fabric of her life, but in every instance, the silver thread gleamed brighter.

There was a night, years later, when she stood beneath streetlights that flickered in the rain. She was older by then, yet still searching. The light bounced off puddles at her feet, creating fractured patterns that reminded her of those childhood storms. The sky above was the same deep gray she remembered, but this time, she stood unafraid. The silver streaks were not just behind her—they were a part of her now.

The concept of silver streaks defined not only her journey but also the message she carried for others. The silver streaks became symbols of hope in every story she shared, whether from a stage, in a song, or across the worn pages of journals she kept. They were not moments that erased pain but ones that re-framed it—reminding her and those who listened that beauty could be born from even the most shattered places.

She often said that silver was a color forged, reflective yet resilient through fire. It was not gold, bright and unblemished, but something stronger—able to bend without breaking. That was the essence of her story.

This memoir is not a collection of tragedies or uninterrupted victories. It is a map of the winding road that became her life, marked by moments where light pressed through the cracks. In telling her story, she extends an invitation to those still waiting for their silver streaks to appear.

For the reader, this journey offers more than inspiration. It serves as a reminder that the storms of life are often accompanied by flashes of silver—brief, brilliant, and capable of altering the landscape. Sometimes, all it takes is a single streak of light to change the course of a life.

Now, as she steps into a new chapter, Silver Streak Lady no longer waits for silver streaks to find her. She chases them. Every performance, every word spoken aloud, every act of kindness is another streak of silver left in her wake. Her story continues to unfold, and in doing so, she becomes part of the light that guides others through their storms.

Her song—rooted in pain but lifted by hope—echoes across the following pages. And if you listen closely, you might hear it, like the faint hum of a melody rising in the distance.

That melody began long before she knew how to name it. It rose like vapor from cracked concrete, delicate yet persistent, in moments when silence could have easily swallowed her whole.

As a child, she often hummed under her breath, the vibrations barely escaping her lips as she rocked herself to sleep on thin mattresses in unfamiliar rooms. It was the kind of sound born from longing—a longing for safety, love, and a place to belong.

The homes she drifted through during those years never held music the way she did. The walls were stark, the floors bare, but she carried melodies inside her ribcage, small flickers of light warming the coldest spaces. Her brothers often laughed when she sang, teasing her with playful jabs about becoming the next Diana Ross. But even their laughter couldn't erase how singing made her feel—as if she belonged somewhere briefly, even if that place existed only in the notes that danced through her chest.

She remembered one particular evening when the power had gone out in the foster home. The darkness was thick, wrapping around her like a heavy cloak, and the other children whispered nervously in the next room. She sat alone by the window, staring at the faint glow of distant streetlights. Without thinking, she began to hum. It started softly at first, a fragile thread weaving through the dark, but it grew as she sang familiar hymns learned from church. Her voice wasn't polished but held a raw purity that filled the emptiness around her.

By the time the power returned, the room felt warmer, as if the song had left traces of light behind.

That was the first time she understood the power of silver streaks—not as literal beams of light but as small acts of resilience capable of transforming the atmosphere.

Years later, she often remembered those quiet moments when she stood on larger stages beneath dazzling lights. Something was grounding about remembering the simplicity of her beginnings. The audience might see a confident woman with a microphone in hand, but behind the glamour lived the echoes of a little girl singing to the darkness, praying it would soften its grip.

Silver Streak Lady's story was not one of instant triumph. For every stage she graced, nights were spent questioning whether she could continue. There were seasons when the silver streaks dimmed, almost disappearing beneath layers of grief and exhaustion. But even in those times, the hum of that childhood melody would return, lifting her just enough to continue moving forward.

Her faith played no small part in that persistence. She often opened a weathered Bible in the quiet hours, tracing the underlined verses that had become lifelines. Isaiah 54:4 was one she returned to repeatedly— "Do not be afraid; you will not suffer shame. Do not fear disgrace; you will forget the shame of your youth." The words resonated deeply as if written directly for her.

When she sang those scriptures aloud, they transformed into songs of hope, and in those moments, she could feel the silver thread of redemption weaving through her heart.

There were performances that Silver Streak Lady never forgot—not because of the crowd or applause but because of the faces she glimpsed beyond the stage. In one small church, she noticed an older woman sitting in the back, her eyes wet with tears as she listened. After the service, the woman approached and held her hands tightly, whispering, "I heard my own story in your song."

Encounters like that reminded her why she continued to sing, even when the weight of her past threatened to pull her under. Her voice had become more than her own; it belonged to those who had forgotten how to speak hope into their lives.

On another occasion, during a benefit concert for survivors of domestic violence, she met a young girl no older than ten. The child stood silently in the corner, clutching a small stuffed animal. After the performance, the girl tugged at her sleeve and simply said, "I like your silver hair." Something in her eyes spoke of unspoken burdens, and Silver Streak Lady knelt to whisper, "You have silver streaks, too. You can't see them yet."

That night, the woman reflected on the invisible streaks others carried—the burdens hidden beneath smiles, the scars concealed by polite laughter. If her music could lighten even one person's shadows, every step of her journey would have been worth it.

As time passed, the silver streaks became more than symbolic. They were part of how she carried herself through the world. Where others saw brokenness, she saw reflections of beauty. Where some counted losses, she counted the silver threads stitched into the fabric of their lives.

It wasn't that the pain disappeared; some wounds left marks too deep to fade fully. But like the Japanese art of Kintsugi—where cracks in pottery are filled with gold to highlight the beauty of imperfection— her story bore witness to the strength found in broken places.

She began to encourage others to see their silver streaks. "Your life," she would say, "isn't defined by the darkness you've walked through but by the light that broke through it."

Silver Streak Lady's story continues to unfold. Even now, her song stretches into the corners of rooms where shadows linger. She stands not as someone who has reached the end of her path but as someone who walks alongside others, still searching for their streaks of light.

This memoir is not an ending—it is a beginning. It is an offering to those who believe their stories are too heavy to carry alone. Through the following pages, Silver Streak Lady invites readers to find their voice, sing through the darkness, and chase after the silver streaks that wait just beyond the clouds.

If you listen closely, you will hear the hum of a song that began long ago, rising with each silver flash that dances across the sky.

CONTENTS

CHAPTER 1
CHILDHOOD BUGABOOS

Puff... wow.

There I was, standing barefoot on the cold aluminum floor, my round brown eyes wide open, wondering if the flames on the stove were going to come and get me. My hero—my big brother—somehow always knew how to control those flames, even though he jumped back as if he were in a fight with them. In my little mind, it was a battle, and I watched closely. He was eight. I was not quite two.

Suddenly, there was a knock on the faded wooden door, and the whole morning shifted. It felt strange—heavy somehow. I could hear my other brother screaming,

"I want my bike! I want my bike! I want my bike!"

My hero was now in a shouting match with strangers. Swiftly, he picked me up, grabbed our infant brother, and in the middle of chaos, we were rushed into a car—a four-door blue and silver Cadillac sedan.

My brother was still screaming for his bike as I sat on my older brother's lap, tears streaming down my chubby cheeks. I stared out the window, my little heart pounding so hard I thought it would burst from my chest.

A strange woman tried to console my screaming brother while the other two children sat quietly, their mouths full of chocolate candy. All six of us were crammed into that car.

As soon as the candy was gone, the screaming began again.

"Where's my mommy? I want my bike!"

You'd think, being the only girl, I would have been Miss Diva — but no. I was too busy observing, analyzing, and, of course, inwardly singing. That was my norm, even in the middle of trauma, because that's what my momma taught me from the womb — there was always a song.

But where was she now?

Still, I looked out the window, my tear-filled, round, cheeky brown eyes searching. Yet somehow — whether in the past, present, or future — there was always a song.

And in that moment, the song rose quietly within me:

I feel so all alone,
I feel so all alone.
Does anybody understand
The questions in my mind,
Destroying my world of peace?
My little heart — it was so sublime.
Paralyzing my soul,
Shaken by mobility...
Du du du... du du du...
They took away my hope,
Leaving no stability.
Du du du alone...
Du du du alone...
So all alone.
Can't you see?
Can't you feel?
So all alone.
DU DU DU DU DU DU DU — alone
DU DU DU DU — alone
Oh my mind, my heart — where's the hope?
It shook my soul.
So all alone.
So all alone.
DU DU DU DU DU DU DU DU DU — alone, alone...

"There she is, all right. Now sing it, mini Diana Ross!"

At four years old, having memorized all her songs and moves on the dining room table, those were fun days for me. I was not only performing

— I was acting out something much deeper, though I did not yet understand what.

What began as innocent imitation slowly became something else.

I remember being taken down old cellar stairs late at night. I cannot clearly recall whether I was carried or walked on my own. Much of what followed has remained blurred — as if my mind protected me by closing certain doors.

What I do remember is fear.

I remember the damp air. The thick cobwebs. The heaviness.

And later, as I grew older, I understood what that cellar truly represented.

It was not just a place beneath the house.

It was the place where my innocence was violated.

Being a step ahead during my childhood in learning how to deal with rejection—while remaining grounded in God's Word—made a significant difference in my life. Even as a child, I understood rejection. I immediately related to figures like Moses, Joseph, David, and Jesus—each of whom had experienced rejection before stepping into purpose.

I created a dream world I often retreated into, especially when I could relate to the characters unfolding in my real life. Though I was forced to attend church, it eventually became a part of me—particularly through the experience of Vacation Bible School.

I learned to serve early on. I helped set up tables, chairs, and props, and I stayed afterward to clean up, putting everything back in its place. Serving gave me a sense of belonging—something I longed for but never fully received at the foster home.

The rewards of serving were quiet but lasting. They led me to seek and depend on favor—not from people, but from God. The church family cheered me on far more than my foster family ever did.

Except for the oldest foster sibling. He became a kind of hero to me. I could see that he gave his best and did his part, yet he didn't receive as much recognition as the middle and youngest foster siblings, Monty and Martha.

I learned early on to see life from the underdog's perspective. Ted never gave up. He always went the extra mile and constantly wore a smile, though I could feel the heavy weight he carried—the longing for real love and the quiet pain in his heart.

Because of him, compassion began to grow in me. I slowly turned away from hate, abandoning the ritual of poking pins into a doll in fits of rage against anyone who hurt me.

I had been given a strange-looking doll—one I thought was ugly—just as I had often been told I was ugly by the youngest foster sibling. She would tell me to go play in my room, where I "belonged," and to mind my own business. She was eight years older than I was and would retaliate anytime I received recognition. She would grab my arm and dig her long, cat-like nails into my skin until it bled.

I was defiant. I refused to cry.

We weren't allowed to tattle, so I couldn't report the abuse. My anger and rage built quietly over time until one day I finally slapped her hard enough to end the ordeal. After that, when I began receiving attention from the oldest sibling, she slowly withdrew from her vicious behavior. The pin-poking stopped. The outward hatred subsided.

But the bitter, uncontrollable crying continued—night after night.

I didn't know how to stop the feeling of wanting to die.

Even though I had the church family cheering me on and my big foster brother offering empathy, I still felt overwhelmingly lonely. The terrible nightmares were constant—the evil laughter in my ears, the visions of running away, and the sensation of falling, only to wake up shaking violently.

I felt as if I were constantly fighting off the faces of demons.

Eventually, those visions faded for a while, but I never told anyone about the episodes. I was afraid it would be considered tattling. At the time, I had no understanding of spiritual warfare, yet those experiences kept me alert—hyper-aware of both seen and unseen battles.

I began channeling my anger inward through reflection and by comparing myself to the Bible characters who had faced rejection and betrayal. Joseph became my anchor—his dreams, his endurance, and the way he rose above rejection resonated deeply within me.

Over time, I turned rejection and pain into a kind of survival game. I decided I would live like the heroes I read about in Scripture. I retreated into a make-believe world where I imagined myself becoming like those biblical figures who fascinated me far more than Dorothy from The Wizard of Oz, Cinderella, Mary Poppins, or even the characters from West Side Story.

And when the darkness would creep up my body like a heavy blanket—paralyzing me with fear—I felt as though death itself was trying to overtake me.

But I soon learned that even the thought of Jesus would cause that deathly presence to disintegrate. I remember that experience happening at least three times—always at night.

The "death angel" never succeeded.

Yet another hidden force in my life remained—molestation.

Being raised not to speak unless spoken to kept me from revealing what was really happening to me. That enforced silence dulled my fight-or-flight instincts, not only in childhood but in later years as well.

The denial of my own voice left deep scars that would shape much of my life.

It wasn't a one-time incident. It happened again and again.

Each time, I learned to stand still.

Each time, I swallowed my tears.

Each time, I told myself I was strong.

I finally found the courage to tell my favorite cousin, Mary, what was happening to me. She was devastated.

Because of the fear that had built up inside me — convinced there was a boogeyman lurking around the house — I wet the bed almost every night until I was eight years old. I was terrified to walk outside alone to the outhouse tool shed in the dark.

The foster mother made sure my wet mattress was placed outside where visitors and friends could see it. It was her way of humiliating me — proof, she thought, of my weakness.

I didn't realize how fast I could run or hide until I was eight years old — the day I received the licking of my life.

I had accidentally broken the half-tilted antenna on my foster father's 1957 Chevy. I loved fixing things. I was always meddling with something in the house. Most of the time, when something broke, I somehow managed to repair it. It surprised even me.

I remembered watching my brother try to fix the television. He became frustrated and gave up. The next day, curiosity got the best of me. I decided to try — and to my surprise, I made it work.

So why not fix that antenna? I had fixed so many things before. I believed I could make it better than it had been.

But when I attempted to repair it, the antenna snapped off completely.

My heart dropped to the ground.

I knew there was going to be an explosion.

Something big was about to happen.

Panicking, I tried to prop the antenna back into place, tilting it carefully with fear and trembling hands. When it wouldn't stay, I ran and hid.

It felt like I was hiding for hours.

Finally, my cousin found me and said my foster dad wanted to see me. We both tried to reassure each other — surely it wouldn't be that bad. I had tried my best to fix it.

But as I walked toward the dining room, a chilling voice echoed inside me:

This is it. You might even die today.

All six faces were watching. Their expressions were heavy, tense. But my foster father's face — that was something else. It looked like death.

He grabbed my arm.

Before I could react, he began beating me with the three-pound metal antenna.

I screamed.

Everyone started shouting, "Stop! Stop!"

I vaguely remember seeing blood. That image froze inside me.

Somehow, I jolted free from his grip and ran — like a flash of lightning.

Afterward, I crawled into my secret hideaway and stayed there for hours, singing silently inside my heart, trying to push the pain away.

You're probably wondering about that hideaway.

Nature has a way of welcoming broken children — and it had already begun preparing a refuge for me, even before that day.

The neighborhood kids often came to our yard because it was the largest in the area...

As we were playing kickball one afternoon, Skippy kicked the ball straight into the thick lilac bushes. I dropped to my stomach to reach it, pushing aside branches and leaves.

That's when I saw it.

Tucked inside the lilacs was the most unusual arrangement of flowers. Lily of the valley — my favorite — growing where they had no business growing, right in the middle of those bushes.

The aroma was heavenly.

That hidden cluster became my peace in the valley.

Not long after that, my foster dad disappeared from the home. For years, I carried a quiet guilt, wondering if it was somehow my fault.

Life shifted again.

I became Cinderella. Snow White. All of the above.

The chores multiplied, and so did the insults. I was called ugly. Stupid. Worthless. Those words echoed longer than the sound of any beating ever could.

Spring and fall meant deep cleaning — inside and out. Mopping. Sweeping. Dusting. Ironing. Outside, I pushed the old-fashioned grass cutter across the yard, then later the hand mower — over two acres of land.

Winter was the hardest.

Shoveling wet, heavy snow. Then dry, biting snow. Making pathways from the front door to the back door. From the front door to the mailbox. From the front door to the driveway. From the back door to the trailer in the yard.

I was eight years old.

(It's interesting now, thinking about how my Papi had to provide for his family at eight. Trauma has a way of repeating itself in different forms.)

Mary, my favorite foster cousin, stopped coming around after witnessing the beating I received. It traumatized her.

But before she pulled away, she made sure I had her beautiful, classy, stylish clothes whenever they no longer fit her. I will always remember the favor I had with my cousin Mary — especially after one of the worst Christmases of my life.

I hurried to unwrap a bright, colorful package from my foster mom and the youngest sibling. They were watching me closely, waiting for my reaction. I could hardly contain my excitement.

Layer by layer, I peeled away the pink tissue paper.

There, lying flat in the box, was an old, gray, tattered sweater.

"What's the matter, Evelyn? Don't you like the sweater? It's for ugly, stupid girls like you."

They stared at me.

In that moment, I wished the floor would open and swallow me whole. My heart felt crushed into pieces. But instead of crying, I smiled. I shrugged it off.

Their faces fell — confused, disappointed. They had expected tears.

That incident reminded me of the little Osgood girls in the neighborhood — girls who were less fortunate than I was and often picked on at school for wearing torn and tattered clothes.

That so-called gift shifted something inside me.

It made me think about their shame.

It made me more sensitive.

I began giving away the best of my old clothes — the ones that no longer fit me — so they would have something nice to wear.

Of course, that caused me to be picked on too.

So I shrugged that off as well.

Looking back, that season shaped me. It taught me never to forget the rejected ones in my space.

But later in life, I also learned something harder:

Not everyone who is hurting is ready to be helped.

So I continually escaped pain — and its scars — by immersing myself in church functions: hayrides, making decorations for parade floats where our church was proudly represented, roller skating, snow sledding, Vacation Bible School, and religious instruction classes.

Church became my refuge.

From time to time, I would watch my friends leave those events with their families, laughing and walking hand in hand. I would wonder what it felt like to belong to a real family.

Somewhere deep inside, I began to sense that the Jones family was not my real family — and maybe that was why they couldn't love me as their own.

So I learned not to expect love.

In fact, by the age of four, I had already grasped the difference between obligation and love.

I reminded myself of that often, especially during the nights when the bitter, uncontrollable crying would not stop.

I didn't know how to silence the overwhelming feeling of wanting to die.

So I fought what I later came to understand as an orphan spirit — clinging to hope that one day I would find my real family.

At the age of ten, my fragile world of hope shattered.

My heart was crushed into pieces.

I couldn't express what I was feeling.

When I found out that my biological mother had died, that news struck me harder than learning I had five brothers and two sisters — information that felt distant and blurry.

My four younger brothers were separated and placed two by two into different foster homes.

My oldest brother was placed with the two youngest boys, but he was blamed for much of the trouble and eventually sent to Boys' Industry outside of Rochester, New York.

I fell into a deep depression.

I had always dreamed of finding my real mother. I knew I was different. I knew I didn't belong to the Jones family.

My grades began to drop, and I was on the verge of failing fifth grade.

That same year, the Gideons handed out Bibles at school. I still remember receiving mine.

That Bible became my best friend.

Whenever I felt lonely or confused, I turned to it. Whenever I had questions, I searched its pages for answers.

Meanwhile, Mrs. Jones brought in another foster sister around my age. Her name was Evelyn too, but everyone called her Peaches.

Peaches didn't stay long.

She didn't like what she saw and quickly moved to another foster home. For her, life in the boondocks with the Jones family — and with me — was too boring.

But while she was there, she brought laughter into a serious and secluded atmosphere. She was fun. She was hilarious. And for a brief moment, she brought light into my world.

One scripture became my anchor:

Psalm 27:10

"When my father and my mother forsake me, then the LORD will take me up."

I don't believe my mother and father intended to forsake me.

The foster system came and took all six of us at once. There was no intervention from our grandmother, Ruby Mae Wilkerson.

My mother, Jessie, and my grandmother had been estranged for years.

From what I was told, my mother had my baby brother and me with the same Puerto Rican man — better known as Paco, my Papi.

Years later, when I finally had the chance to speak with him, I asked what it was that made him fall in love with her.

He smiled and said, "She was beautiful... and she could cook!"

After my baby brother was born, they eventually went their separate ways. He later told me that if he had known she was in abusive relationships, he would have rescued her. He never believed in laying a hand on a woman. He deeply loved his mother, his baby sister, and his brother — and from the age of eight, he had to help support them after his own father deserted the family.

He always wondered what happened to his baby girl — the one he named — and to his son, whom he named after himself.

Later in life, I learned that Puerto Rican culture is deeply rooted in close-knit family bonds. Family is everything.

One passage carried me through those years:

Psalm 23

The Lord is my Shepherd; I shall not want.

He makes me lie down in green pastures;

He leads me beside the still waters.

He restores my soul.
He leads me in paths of righteousness for His name's sake.
Yea, though I walk through the valley of the shadow of death,
I will fear no evil; for You are with me;
Your rod and Your staff, they comfort me.
You prepare a table before me in the presence of my enemies;
You anoint my head with oil; my cup runs over.
Surely goodness and mercy shall follow me all the days of my life,
And I will dwell in the house of the Lord forever.

Soon, I had almost forgotten that I had a deceased biological mother and seven siblings. I became absorbed in hayrides, church functions, picking fruit, and going to carnivals — anything that felt alive.

Even though I saw my six siblings twice after our mother's funeral at what we called "mini reunions," my interest slowly faded. My visits with my baby sister, which had been twice a month, eventually dwindled to once a month.

Somewhere inside, I was protecting myself.

And when the ache became too heavy, I went to my garden.

My Musical Garden
My Musical Garden
Far from the pain — what's there to gain?
In my beautiful, beautiful, beautiful garden,
Yes, my Musical Garden.
My Musical Garden,
My Musical Garden —
The flowers tell me,
"This is where your pain is set free."
In my beautiful, beautiful, beautiful garden.

CHAPTER TWO
TEEN NUISANCES

At the age of thirteen, I learned that our biological mother had been shot and murdered while visiting my baby sister's foster home on the weekends. At the time, I couldn't fully grasp the weight of what murder truly meant. I had lived such a secluded life that violence and death were foreign concepts to me, barely registering in my mind.

As a teenager, I wasn't allowed to do many of the things my friends did—like going to movies or parties. But even then, I wasn't particularly interested in those things. After playing the cornet at football games and being part of the marching band for three years, I quit. I had witnessed a horrible fight that left a defenseless player with a broken collarbone, and that trauma was enough for me.

I never bragged about the bloody bathroom incident, but it proved a point. I was very angry—often unable to express myself, let alone speak my mind. Cursing was out of the question in our house. Mrs. Jones usually didn't come into the bathroom, but that day she must have sensed something. Like many mothers, I felt she had eyes in the back of her head.

I had told her that she didn't love me or understand me. The next thing I knew, there was blood in the sink, on the floor, and even on the toilet seat.

Looking into her eyes, I said,

"You shed the blood — you clean it."

I don't know what expression I wore, but it must have been enough, because she backed up and quickly left the bathroom.

I washed my face, went to school, and acted as if nothing had happened. I had learned to mask my trauma well. Our home wasn't a place for discussing feelings — or anything related to real life.

When I got home that afternoon, the bathroom was spotless. Mrs. Jones was unusually quiet, and so was I. I had forgotten that my social worker, Mrs. Smith, was due to visit that week.

Later, as I sat on the couch in silence, Mrs. Smith asked,

"So, Evelyn, how are things going?"

"So-so, I guess," I replied.

"Well, have you thought about what you'd like to be when you grow up?"

"Yes," I said. "I'd like to be a policewoman and kill everyone who gets in my way."

Mrs. Smith looked at me, her face pale with shock.

"Evelyn, I don't think you mean that. Is there something bothering you? Are you upset about something?"

"Yes, Mrs. Smith!" I answered.

"And why is that, Evelyn?" she asked.

Well, it seems like I can't do anything. I can't go to church outings. There's a camp trip coming up, and I'm not allowed to go. No movies, no sleepovers with classmates... nothing!"

Mrs. Smith turned to Mrs. Jones.

"Is that true?"

"Yes," Mrs. Jones replied. "It's for her own protection."

"Mrs. Jones, a church camp outing would be a great experience for Evelyn. I think she should go. As for the sleepovers, you can just make sure they're chaperoned."

"So, Evelyn," Mrs. Smith said, turning back to me, "you're going to camp, and we want you to have a great time. I'm sure it will be a life-changing experience."

"Thank you, Mrs. Smith! I'll let my pastor know I can go to Camp Asbury!"

"You're welcome, Evelyn," Mrs. Smith replied. "And I hope you consider a new, happier career for your future."

"Also... I'd like to meet my biological father."

Oh wow — I struck another nerve. All the blood drained from Mrs. Smith's face.

"Well, I'll have to work on that, Evelyn..."

With that, she quickly got up and left — very frazzled.

As time passed, I eagerly awaited Camp Asbury, which was scheduled in about a week.

As I gathered my thoughts about what I would share at Camp Asbury—whether a testimony or a prayer request—I reflected on my childhood and early teen years. In doing so, I realized something profound about the abuse I had endured.

I'm not sure what was worse: getting spankings for telling the truth or for lying. Either way, I was always in trouble. Or perhaps enduring emotional, mental, psychological, and spiritual torment from ages eight to seventeen was worse.

On top of the spankings, I had to pick my own switch. And if it wasn't the kind that stung, Big Momma Jones would find one that did.

I believed Big Momma Jones showed her love through strict discipline. However, with Mrs. Jones—her daughter-in-law—it felt more like obligation. She probably felt stuck with me after Big Momma passed away when I was four years old.

Daily—whether at church, school, or home—I felt a constant shadow looming over me.

But then Camp Asbury arrived.

The best moment was at the cozy campfire, where we were invited to release our darkness and fears. It was time to let go of the overcast shadow that had haunted me.

As we shared our stories, mine seemed the most dramatic. They gathered around me and prayed. Immediately, the anxiety and fear lifted.

Those around me cheered as they saw a smile—and tears of joy—stream down my face.

I felt an indescribable warmth inside and out, beyond any heat the campfire could offer, penetrating the cold air on that dark night.

On my way back, I decided to cherish everything I felt and resolved to share my excitement only with my friends. I would have to contain it until I got to school—which felt like an eternity.

I still struggled with paranoia about my conversations with Mrs. Jones. She often squashed them, especially if I showed any excitement. One time, I got grounded for simply saying that Greg Morris from Mission: Impossible was a good-looking man. To her, that was being fresh.

So, my friends were the ones who heard about my experiences at Camp Asbury, and they could clearly see the dramatic impact it had on me. I truly appreciated how they never gave up on breaking down the walls I built from time to time.

After another period of being grounded, my school friends, Mary and Melinda, noticed a change in my demeanor. Normally bubbly, I had become withdrawn. It took them three days to break through my barriers.

How could I explain my deep-seated fears about murder—a subject never discussed in my foster home? I'm sure they had experienced natural deaths in their families. But could they truly comprehend the profound psychological impact of murder?

Soon, I started working part-time. I hardly had any time for my friends, but they understood my schedule.

After school, my first job was caring for Mrs. Bates for a few hours each afternoon, making sure she took her medicine after lunch. I could hardly wait to get to her house just to hear her stories. She had a gentle spirit, and I looked forward to seeing her every day.

It ended sadly when she passed away, but her granddaughter later told me how much joy I had brought to her in her final days. That encounter was bittersweet. After her death, I decided I couldn't bear to care for the elderly again. Losing her felt too personal.

About a week after Mrs. Bates' passing, I rushed off the bus one afternoon, knowing I had chores to finish before Bible study that evening.

As I stepped inside and closed the door behind me, I glanced over and noticed the youngest foster sibling and Mrs. Jones looking through a family photo album. Curious, I quickly joined them.

"Where are my baby pictures?" I asked.

Without hesitation, Mrs. Jones replied cruelly,

"You were so ugly that we didn't take any pictures of you."

The words stung deeply, but I concealed my pain. Later, I found comfort and affirmation from my pastor and his wife. They reminded me of my inherent worth and pointed me to Psalm 139:14:

"I praise You, for I am fearfully and wonderfully made."

I learned to channel my thoughts and focus on helping others who might be less fortunate than I was in whatever struggles they faced.

There was a young boy, about ten years old, named Tommy. I cared about him deeply and often encouraged him to know God. Though others labeled him a troublemaker, I believed he was simply trying to get attention. Beneath his goofiness, Tommy had a serious side. We related to each other in many ways.

One day, his family was moving furniture. He was sitting on the back of the truck, trying to hold the furniture down, when he accidentally fell. He hit his head and died instantly.

I was heartbroken. He was so young. I was sick over it for a long time. Just days before the accident, I had found out that Tommy had decided to let Jesus into his heart. That brought me some comfort, but I still missed him deeply.

Amid these trials, I faced a grave situation involving a local truck driver that escalated into an assault. The trauma left me shaken and questioning my safety and self-worth. At home, issues like this were never discussed. Silence surrounded anything painful or inappropriate.

Shortly afterward, I became terrified that I might be pregnant. I was still so young, and my fear of childbirth had been shaped by dramatic television scenes that left lasting impressions on me. The possibility filled me with dread.

While in the eighth grade, I recall being the "star" in a class project titled A Black Student in an All-White School. Interestingly, it never dawned on me that, from kindergarten through twelfth grade, I had simply been living my life — not as a statement, not as a symbol — but as myself.

Racism was not tolerated in our town. Even though the title of that project suggested otherwise, across the board there was no open hostility allowed. I was treated as part of the community, and everyone knew everyone. If someone crossed a line, it was handled quickly.

I do remember one incident on the bus. A boy muttered the "n" word under his breath as I stepped off. The next day, he showed up with a black eye and his arm in a sling. As I passed him, one of the neighborhood boys leaned over and said, "Hey Evie, if he ever calls you that name again, just let us know." I was puzzled — I hadn't realized anyone else had even heard him.

The foster family I lived with was in an all-white community, yet respect was understood. That incident became the talk of the town for weeks.

We, as "Negros," were often seen as excelling in singing, dancing, sports, music, and acting. Although I remember having to leave choir rehearsal alone one day because I didn't project my voice enough.

Ironically, during choir rehearsal, I was once asked to leave because I didn't project my voice loudly enough. That moment hit me deeply. I walked out alone.

It wasn't just about singing.

It was rejection — and rejection had always been my most sensitive trigger.

I wanted to crawl under a chair rather than walk down those steps off the stage — then walk the full length of it and another ten feet before disappearing through those heavy doors.

So instead, I poured myself into the school band. Of all instruments, I chose the cornet — the one that had been hidden away in the house.

There was a piano sitting in plain sight, but I wasn't encouraged to play it. I didn't push the issue. I rarely pushed anything.

I was called a "Jesus Freak" and sometimes even a "Holy Roller." It didn't faze me much. I had a Jewish-Christian best friend and a few others who stood by me. Even the high school principal supported us — he allowed us to use his private office for prayer. That meant more than he probably knew.

Interestingly, the one who bullied me the most later became something of an evangelist. It shocked many students. Several of the guys said I had been a strong influence on him, even though he had once been the ringleader in calling me names. He went on to touch many lives — and then, tragically, he died in a car accident.

From time to time, I escaped into the simple joys of youth. I loved hayrides, especially the hot chocolate afterward — warm, sweet, and comforting against the cold night air. We also spent days and evenings crafting thousands of Kleenex roses for parade floats, a tradition that lasted three years.

Afterward, we celebrated with ice cream treats — banana splits and hot fudge sundaes — a sweet continuation of the community gatherings I had loved since I was eleven.

I became passionate about teaching Sunday school at the only United Methodist Church a quarter mile down the road in our village. With creativity and enthusiasm, I easily kept twelve youngsters, ages five to thirteen, engaged and excited for each Sunday. The only daunting task was lighting the massive church furnace an hour before service to heat the building. That part intimidated me every time.

When my favorite pastor — the one who had known me since I was two years old — prepared to leave, I felt a deep sadness. But she reassured me that her successor would be wonderful.

The new lay pastor and his family were inspiring. He introduced me to Lay Witness Mission trips beyond our small town, expanding my world far past pajama parties and local outings.

Miraculously, I was allowed to go on Lay Witness Missions with my lay pastor twice during those two summers. We traveled as far as Hershey, Pennsylvania — near the New York border — where I witnessed something powerful: seven different denominational churches in one community coming together to worship in one church.

It was also on those trips that I had my first encounter with cockroaches and mice. Ironically, I had once laughed at someone who experienced that for the first time. I quickly learned a humbling lesson — never laugh at someone else's trial, because you may soon walk through a similar one yourself.

Having grown so accustomed to being secluded and overprotected, the thought of permanently leaving the small hamlet of Fowlerville was unthinkable. You could blink your eye and pass straight through town. The nearest store was five miles away, and my school was seven.

Even though I had been told that once I turned eighteen, I was on my own — that I would have to fend for myself — the reality felt terrifying. The statistics for foster youth aging out of the system are staggering. Nearly half face homelessness within the first eighteen months. By then, I had learned to depend on God as best I knew how — though it was often a zeal without wisdom, something that would soon unravel.

There were those butterflies again — stronger than ever — mixed with anxiety and excitement filling my body. Just knowing I had been accepted to Bible school in East Providence, Rhode Island, felt unbelievable.

I turned nineteen in July and began classes that September. From nineteen to twenty-two, I attended a three-year accredited Bible school and lived on campus.

Those three years were eye-opening.

For the first time, I was told I wasn't "Black enough." That comment stunned me. Yet during three months of nonstop revival meetings, being Spirit-filled and immersed in worship and prayer, I was unknowingly being prepared for inner-city ministry.

In the natural, coming from the quiet boondocks was no match for the gang-filled projects of Providence, Rhode Island. And just when I thought that was intense, another turn in my journey placed me in the Bronx, New York City.

Thank God for the three times hands were laid on me by the Chancellor of the Bible School, Dr. Heroo. Apparently, he saw something in me that I did not yet see in myself. He even called me his "shouting corner." At the end of the year, he presented medallions to twelve of his favorite students — and by God's grace, I was among them.

Among those I admired during that season were Dr. Heroo, Shambach, and the Shuttlesworth family.

During my internship in the Bronx, one of the most frightening moments came when I was asked to dress as a clown and minister to children on the streets of New York City. The outreach was meant for children who had known little joy — only trauma.

For some reason, they were drawn to me. Being naïve and eager to connect, I befriended them freely. Suddenly, they began pulling on my oversized clown nose and tugging at my costume. Within moments, what began as excitement turned into a stampede-like frenzy. The church adults quickly realized what was happening and rescued me.

Even though I was in disguise, dozens of children were violently tugging at my clown suit in the sweltering summer heat. It was in the high eighties, and I began losing my balance. That was a summer I would never forget.

As my internship continued, my prophetic gifting began to manifest more clearly, and my musical talent found greater expression in street meetings and church gatherings alike.

One of the most challenging assignments I faced during my second summer was mentoring Moses — the influence of a youth cell group of about sixteen members. Their original leader was preparing to leave, and the group felt discouraged and uncertain. Moses felt the weight of their expectations. They looked up to him, yet he felt unprepared to lead.

I took him aside and spoke into his life, encouraging him to step fully into what God had already placed within him.

The following week, I was in for a surprise.

As the former leader stepped down and I returned, Moses walked in — not with sixteen youth, but with sixty-six. Sixty-six young people came with him, energized and encouraged. The growth from 16 to 66 so impressed the pastor that he placed me over the management of the youth services in addition to assisting in the main services.

That season stretched me.

My first summer of internship had already introduced me to a different kind of awakening.

Coming out of the boondocks into the Bronx was culture shock in every sense of the word. I went from a predominantly white rural community to a Puerto Rican and Black urban neighborhood filled with life, rhythm, and struggle.

That first summer, I was placed in children's ministry.

During the Fourth of July holiday, the church ministered in the streets — handing out food, organizing games — and I was assigned to sing. Fireworks exploded overhead. Street hustling buzzed around us. I stood there shaking inside, butterflies storming in my stomach.

Yet as I sang, blocking out the noise, something happened.

It felt as though everything stopped.

People were hanging out of their windows. The talking and yelling ceased. Even the personal fireworks stopped.

It felt like the Twilight Zone.

As my voice rang out into the night, it seemed to echo into infinity.

The second summer, they needed to replace the youth director — and they chose me. Some felt I was too soft-spoken for the role. Until I poured into one teenager who, within one week, brought sixty-six teenagers — up from sixteen.

It was a challenging season, but powerful. The new youth began turning their lives to Jesus. I never saw the jealousy coming. I was too focused on lives being changed.

What eventually got me removed — though the pastor fought on my behalf — was pressured. He gave way to the accuser.

I was accused of taking the youth group to see the movie Grease, which was considered forbidden. I had permission, but the noise against me grew louder. One of the youth later confirmed that the very person accusing me was watching R- and X-rated movies in their own home.

The youth wanted me to expose the hypocrisy.

But I didn't believe in confrontation.

So I stepped aside.

And I watched God show up and show out.

My focus during my final semester at Bible School was to fully embrace the powerful revivals that swept through that year. The most unforgettable was with Evangelist R.W. Schambach.

I remember him declaring,

"Just throw them outside — the Spirit is so high they won't even realize they're in the snow!"

I made up my mind that I would be one of the last ones standing.

"I'm not going to be thrown outside," I told myself.

Well... I was second to the last.

The next person in line was a large woman, and I later learned that Evangelist Schambach was concerned she might fall on me. I heard him say,

"Oh no — get her up! Get her off that little one, please!"

From what I was told, it only took one man to move her — but it took five men to lift me.

That moment stayed with me.

My final year at Zion Bible School seemed to fly by. I found myself pressing deeper into God, knowing this chapter was closing. When my season as youth leader ended, I wasn't quite sure how to process that transition. Leadership had become part of my identity — and now, I had to release it.

Was there another position for me, or was I meant to step away by faith in another direction?

I knew one thing for certain — I could not return to the foster home, and New York no longer felt like a secure landing place. There was no big-brother influence to lean on anymore. I would have to trust God completely.

After graduation, I returned to the Bronx without a position. I felt distant. Abandoned. Rejected.

Yet I was loved by one person — Momma Taylor.

I was learning something powerful:

Sometimes one is enough.

Though I was no longer included on church staff, my worship and praise did not change. Praise and worship were my breakthrough. They fortified me.

During that season, I learned how to be free— how to love deeply, yet not cling. A few people showed me kindness when I would withdraw during what felt like daily spiritual warfare. That period quietly drew me closer to God, preparing me for a future I could not yet see.

Then, unexpectedly, California was impressed upon my spirit.

I didn't know anyone there. I didn't know how long I would stay, what I would do, or where I would live. But I mentioned it to a few people I trusted. Word traveled quickly, and soon I met a couple who encouraged me to pursue what they believed was God's direction.

They knew of an elderly woman named Margarita who had always loved foster children and adults. She requested that I come stay with her. Even though I was grown, she didn't care — knowing I had come through the foster system was enough for her.

That was where I learned something new: Puerto Ricans and Mexicans did not always see eye to eye. I hadn't even realized they were two different nationalities. My world was expanding in ways I never expected.

Soon after arriving, I found a live-in job caring for eight children — the youngest just eighteen months old and the oldest ten. Life moved quickly. Illnesses, school calls, responsibility. Five of the eight children were sent home sick one week, and suddenly I was fully immersed.

There was no easing into adulthood.

I was in it.

For the children to return to school, both the homeowner and the doctor had to sign a release form. When she refused to sign it promptly, I was advised to leave the job as soon as I received my paycheck.

The main homeowner had scolded me for something that wasn't my fault or my responsibility. Margarita warned me that if things went wrong and the children were reported as neglected, my name could be dragged into it. She was concerned that my reputation could be permanently damaged.

So we made a plan.

I placed my belongings in the garage ahead of time so Margarita could quickly retrieve them. She waited outside while I went in to collect my pay.

The homeowner didn't even want to come out to pay me, but because I remained persistent, she finally appeared with the check and signed the release for the children. She seemed more interested in building another home to take in more children than caring for the five who were already sick in the first one.

After calling me just about every name imaginable, she dismissed me with a laugh.

I calmly thanked her for the check and told her I was leaving.

She didn't realize my belongings were already in the garage.

Margarita moved quickly, loaded everything into the car, and waited for me. When I walked out with my check in hand, we drove away.

While staying with Margarita, there was always company — people coming and going, conversations, laughter, stories. It was a lively home.

And that's when I met a gentleman who began to take interest in me...

He was repulsive and wanted only one thing — my body.

But he wasn't able to get me.

When I asked him if I could pray for him, he immediately withdrew, realizing I wasn't interested in lustful activity. For the last time, I asked again if I could pray for him. That's when he confessed he wasn't ready to give up his lifestyle.

He agreed to sign my Bible and shared stories about his past — how he had once been a right-hand man in the gangs, known as "Little Jo Jo," connected to the era of The Cross and the Switchblade.

That was the end of that chapter.

A week later, I found a job at a bank doing data input. I remembered what my Aunt Jean had always said about how quickly my hands moved across number keys. She was right.

To get to the job, I had to take three buses. Margarita offered to drive me halfway, which made the commute manageable. I was hired.

The woman assigned to train me was a zealous Christian, full of the Holy Spirit. She even offered to pick me up from the second bus stop that brought me into downtown Los Angeles. She told me the color of her car — but I never thought to ask what kind of car it was.

She gave me clear instructions on where to stand at the bus stop and what to look for. When I arrived at that particular spot, I couldn't believe my eyes — stepping out of a small Volkswagen was a six-foot, bubbly Christian sister with the brightest smile.

That was Leslie.

About a month later, I decided to move closer to work so I wouldn't have to take so many buses. Leslie invited me to her church, and I thoroughly enjoyed it. Before I knew it, I was asked to assist with the Young Singles ministry — a division of nearly 500 young adults.

I had never experienced so much genuine love in one place. There was no competition, no jealousy, no coldness. They were devoted to prayer, holy convocations, loving the shut-ins, and seeking God's face.

Meanwhile at work, I was being promoted — three weeks in a row. But along with the promotions came jealousy and competition five days a week. I had even surpassed the department head, who normally received promotions only a couple of times a month. Favor was following me — but so was resistance.

As my internship chapter officially came to a close after the mission in California, I returned to the Bronx and the church that had once felt like home. Many welcomed me warmly — but others did not.

I was prevented from speaking into lives that were clearly shipwrecked — situations I could see unfolding before they collapsed. I was asked to sit in the back of the church, despite being a Zion Bible School alumna.

It was subtle — but it was rejection.

Yet God showed up and showed out.

I didn't fight for position.

I simply showed up — quietly.

And somehow, that made me a threat

SILVER STREAK LADY

(Song Insert — Victorious Tone)

His love shines on you.
His love shines down on you.
You would have never known
what God's love could do.
The sorrow... the pain...
such heartache you went through.
Some people asked,
"What did that pain prove?"_
It proved His grace was stronger.
It proved you were chosen.

It proved you rise.

CHAPTER 3
GROWING THRU IT

Apparently, God was not finished with me here on earth. I am still here—after many car accidents and surviving a domestic violence situation that was finally broken off and removed from my life for good.

That death angel tried to take me out.

But my mother was the one who was shot and murdered during her own domestic cycle. She had looked for love in all the wrong places, having first experienced rejection from her own mother.

Because of prayer—and because I came to know the Word and God personally and consistently—I believe my life was spared. My time was not over.

I was told my mother was a hard worker and a Prayer Warrior. She was the youngest of all her twenty one siblings. Her father was described as the sweetest man—a preacher and a builder–Realtor.

Unfortunately, the grandmother I never knew was said to be deeply wounded and harsh. Only God knows why she was so hardened. Could it have been the toll of bearing twenty-one children? Trauma has a way of reshaping people.

My grandmother's name included "Americus." I was never certain whether that name was given through history, ownership, or something else entirely. There were many unanswered questions.

Interestingly, her parents' last name was Nelson.

My uncle once told me that his mother and father rarely spoke about their upbringing. Silence seemed to run in the family.

Divine Connections

One of the most unexpected Divine connections Growing through it in my life came through dating Greg Morris's nephew — yes, that Greg Morris from Mission Impossible.

Remember when I got grounded for saying Greg Morris was "wuuuuweee soooo fine"? Well, God has a sense of humor.

It was his nephew who later showed me how to create a montage for my very first television show, Explore Your Expectations.

The foundation of that show came from Jeremiah 29:11:

Greg Morris's nephew wore many hats — actor, chef, model — and he helped me create a professional montage for my one-minute TV promo. What once got me grounded for calling Greg Morris "wuuuuweee soooo fine" had now come full circle. God truly does have a sense of humor.

Then, out of nowhere, a Channel 8 news anchor showed up at my church.

While he was speaking with a friend of mine, I was called over and introduced. He looked at me and said, "If there's any way I can help you, let me know."

I tucked that away.

Later that same morning, I began talking with a teenage boy who had been bullied for years. He was a loner — quiet, overlooked. I asked him what he did best.

"I draw," he said. Sketches. Cartoons. Animals.

I asked him if he would draw an eagle for my TV project.

His face lit up.

When he finished, he dedicated the drawings to me. The eagle became symbolic — strength, vision, rising above devastation.

That's when I remembered the news anchor.

I pulled out his contact information and scheduled a meeting at the Channel 8 TV station. He graciously helped me incorporate moments of devastation directly into the eye of the eagle for my montage.

As I focused on my TV Shows I had the phenomenal opportunity to love on The Loved Fugitive - my Papi who was a kingpin and through my song/video, a personal interview with him and having Jeff Fenholt on my show as well as my prayer warrior friend Maria. My Papi turned his life over to the Love of God, Jesus cold turkey of 30+ years of drug trafficking! That's how powerful the blood and love of Jesus/Yeshua is!

Pain transformed into vision.

Ashes into artistry.

Later, through the Jess Anderson Agency, I acted alongside Cuba Gooding Jr. During that four-hour shoot, something happened that startled me. When we finished, he spoke words that almost verbatim echoed the last words my Papi had spoken to me seventeen years earlier.

I froze.

God was weaving threads I couldn't see.

Through that same agency, I was connected to Russ Robinson — Rock Hudson's uncle — who later adopted me as his musical daughter.

From foster rejection...

to divine connections.

From obscurity...

to purpose unfolding.

He trained me well.

One of the first things he taught me was how to shift from writing predominantly in minor melodies — which often reflected my inner sorrow — into stronger major melodic structures. He said, "Your pain has depth, but your victory must have sound."

He served as CEO of The International Songwriters Guild, beginning in Paris, then New York City, and later Orlando, Florida — where our paths crossed.

He allowed me to serve as his assistant and support him in public relations work. For a brief season, I even participated in teen pageants connected to his creative circles.

His résumé was staggering.

He had played piano for Frank Sinatra for over twenty years.

He had received a Purple Heart for his service.

He had been honored internationally and had performed on grand pianos in all fifty states, presidential mansions, commanded four times from the Queen of England,and appeared in more than 120 films.

Being mentored by someone of that caliber expanded my musical vision. For the first time, I saw that excellence and anointing did not have to compete.

Mother Dear," as I lovingly called her, carried her own hidden history.

She had once placed first in casting for an all-Black production of Hello, Dolly! Yet due to family control and pressure from her sister — who had assumed a dominant maternal role — she was not permitted to pursue the opportunity. The role eventually went to Pearl Bailey, who had placed second.

She had also been prevented from singing in the choir of George Jefferson's church — the very church associated with the cultural anthem "Movin' On Up."

Still, her voice did not die.

She wrote a poem honoring Dr. Martin Luther King Jr., a piece so powerful that it was later displayed in the White House. She received personal letters of acknowledgment from multiple Presidents, beginning with President Lyndon B. Johnson and continuing through later administrations.

A meeting had been scheduled for her to meet President Obama, but she passed into glory before that moment could take place.

Her legacy remained.

Her words lived on. "Why Can't We Find Love?" had the privilege of helping her copyright a song she wrote titled Why Can't We Find Love? I also had the honor of taking her into the studio — a moment that felt sacred.

At John Dash Dixon's studio — my music engineer — I gathered three of us ladies to record background vocals alongside her. Watching her step into that recording booth at eighty years old, seventy-five years after first dreaming of singing professionally, felt like witnessing redemption.

What a gift from God.

For her 80th birthday, she fulfilled a childhood dream: to finally record a song in a professional studio. The joy on her face could not be measured. She later distributed her final three CDs among twelve exchange students of different nationalities who had chosen her as Teacher of the Year in Polk County, Florida. Her heart had always embraced diversity. She gave copies to students from Asian, Hawaiian, and African American backgrounds — symbolic of the love she believed the world could one day find.

She had asked me to create videos and help distribute her music more widely, but family dynamics shifted. Wanting to preserve peace, I stepped out of the picture. Sometimes obedience means stepping back, not stepping forward.

During my five years at Pastor Paula White's church in Florida, I encountered remarkable people who helped bring my first CD, Silver Streak Lady, to life. Those five years were nothing short of a divine assignment — a season of stretching, refining, and stepping more fully into my musical calling.

The song Protect the Children was written in fifteen minutes.

I had fallen asleep while waiting for a call from one of the singers, unsure whether they were going to participate. When I woke up, the melody and lyrics flowed almost effortlessly. I had gathered six other artists into the studio, and one renowned artist I met through work turned out to be phenomenal. He played three additional instruments, performed reggae rap, and carried a song close to his heart for twenty-three years. I encouraged him to bring it to the studio and see what would happen.

What unfolded was mind-blowing.

Everyone fell into place as if divinely orchestrated.

You Got It Goin' On, Girl was written in about twenty minutes — a collaboration between the two of us that felt electric and inspired.

Then there was Jessica — a precious young Italian woman in a wheelchair, with the mental capacity of a ten-year-old but a heart full of purity. Working with her brought a tenderness into the studio that cannot be manufactured.

Like an Eagle came together with a beautiful young woman from Belgium named Josie. She followed what I sang in English and responded in a soothing, angelic French melodic voice — all in one take.

Getting her into the studio, however, was like pulling teeth.

Though she followed me faithfully in the church choir, always nearby, she would insist, "No way are you getting me into a studio!"

I promised her I wouldn't make her sing — and technically, I didn't.

But my engineer — who hears nuances like no one I've ever known — captured something extraordinary. What he shaped from that moment was breathtaking.

There were many more songs birthed during that season — stories layered with divine timing, collaboration, and courage — but those will be expounded upon in another book.

At this stage of my music production journey, I realized something about myself — I genuinely enjoyed being in the background.

I loved discovering what made people tick. I loved drawing out what was already inside of them. Those closest to me often encouraged me to put my own voice front and center — after all, that's how the industry usually works. But as I followed God's leading, I sensed He had a different plan.

And His way was far more fulfilling.

It taught me that it was never about me. It was about His Kingdom — about reaching, molding, and challenging the next generation. When you allow God to move through you without striving for personal spotlight, the outcome is far greater than you could orchestrate on your own.

There is something extraordinary about giving others hope, unlocking hidden talents, and creating divine connections through networking.

During that season, the studio became a gathering place for the unlikely and the overlooked:

a seventy-nine-year-old chaplain,

a wheelchair-bound young woman,

three children,

three teenagers,

my cousin,

and a dear friend who had only ever done voice-overs and had never stepped foot inside a recording studio.

There was also a precious young woman from Belgium who simply repeated what I sang in French. She had never recorded before— yet she delivered her part in one flawless take. Off the charts.

Ironically, I — the one accustomed to studio sessions— needed several takes.

Every singer rose to the occasion. Every voice mattered.

That was the beauty of it.

Around that same time, I felt another nudge— California.

I didn't know anyone there. I only remembered hearing that someone on my father's side might live there. I reached out, and to my surprise, we connected. She invited me to visit, and what unfolded from that simple step of faith was both delightful and unexpected.

At that time, I had already been listening to a ministry called the Hollywood Prayer Network, led by Karen Covell. I was even able to attend one of Larry Poland's private breakfast gatherings for celebrities— quietly, under the paparazzi's radar. It stirred something deep inside me.

Then suddenly, an overwhelming and uncontrollable burden came over me for California — and for celebrities.

Two weeks after returning to Florida from California, Pastor Paula White had to travel and would be away for two Sundays. Ironically, both guest speakers that filled in were from California.

Before they even arrived, I sensed God preparing me.

Each Sunday, from the moment the California speakers introduced themselves until they said "Amen," I was undone. Tears streamed down my face. I couldn't contain it. I would rush out of the sanctuary before anyone could see me fully break down.

It wasn't just crying — it was that deep, gut-level, "ugly cry" kind of surrender.

I couldn't explain it logically. I just knew God was dealing with me about California.

The second Sunday was even more intense. The confirmation felt undeniable. It was as though the Spirit was churning something within me that had been waiting to be released.

I didn't know what awaited me in Hollywood. I didn't have a plan. I only knew His heartbeat was California — and I needed to get ready.

When I told my half-sister that I believed God was calling me to move to California within a month, she didn't respond the way I expected. She acted as though she hadn't heard me at all... and then she hung up the phone.

That silence was loud.

But the call was louder.

My stomach dropped and my heart sank. I had no idea where I was going to stay once I arrived — especially after being told it "wouldn't be a problem."

Meanwhile, I had already purchased my bus ticket from Florida to California.

There was no turning back.

God blessed me during that long, tumultuous ride across the country. But once we reached Texas, strange things began happening.

The most bizarre moment occurred in the middle of the night.

A loud thud jolted me awake. A baby was screaming at the top of her lungs. Chaos erupted behind me. The baby's mother began yelling at the grandmother for dropping the child.

Then came the horrifying words:

"Somebody help me! My mom's dead!"

The bus driver quickly pulled over and turned on the lights. As I turned around, I saw the grandmother slumped over, her eyes rolled back.

The driver shouted, "Does anyone know the Heimlich maneuver?"

Within seconds, a passenger jumped up and sprang into action. A piece of candy flew out of her mouth.

She began coughing.

The bus filled with relieved gasps.

She wasn't dead.

She came back to consciousness saying the last thing she remembered was needing something sweet quickly.

Even before that incident, the bus driver had already pulled over once to remove an irrational man who had been screaming and disrupting everyone. He claimed he needed the bathroom, but it was clear something wasn't right.

It felt like spiritual turbulence.

Texas was intense.

But I stayed quiet, praying internally, sensing that the journey to California was not going to be simple — and that opposition often meets obedience.

He had been in a heated argument earlier on the bus — about worshiping trees of all things. Between that disruption and the medical emergency, we arrived nearly five hours late.

California was already proving to be a journey.

I became involved with this ministry for about two years. Master Media International was dynamic, creative, and operated in excellence. It was inspiring to be surrounded by visionaries who believed media could be used for the Kingdom.

At one point, the director felt led to gather fifty members out of the five hundred affiliated with the ministry — a smaller, more intimate celebration. To my surprise, I was chosen as one of the fifty.

During that gathering, we shared fellowship, dreams, testimonies, and personal stories. Somewhere along the journey, I had impacted him — though I never set out to. It was humbling.

Another divine connection along the Kingdom path.

It was there that I met a couple who connected me to one of the most unique music engineers I had ever encountered — Larry Treadwell. He had a way of pulling sound out of you that felt almost dimensional, as if he could hear beyond the notes themselves. Recording with him wasn't technical — it was transformation.

Later, I attended a Stand Up for Jesus–style gathering — a space created so even celebrities could attend freely without paparazzi, without pressure. It was a safe place for worship, prayer, and authenticity.

That's where I met Donna Summer.

She happened to step into the same prayer circle I was standing in. When it came time to share requests, she quietly asked for prayer — but requested that it remain unspoken.

And we honored that.

Another sacred moment. Another divine intersection.

I also met the secretary of John Goodman — known as the voice of Fred Flintstones — and did care giving and intense housework for her. During that time, I had the privilege of saving her life in a critical moment. I loved how God would weave these unexpected divine connections into my journey.

I met a fashion designer who had been set free from childhood bondage. He designed over fifty custom pieces for me. In return, I helped revise his video bio. In just two days, he created a custom Silver Streak Lady dress for an evening TV appearance. It was breathtaking — and symbolic of restoration in both our lives.

While assisting with a media ministry connected to Hollywood Network Connection, I became involved with The 365 Project — producing short films in 365 hours based on a scripture theme.

It was during this time that I met a precious young man whose constant glances eventually led to a surprising discovery — we were actually cousins. His compassion and deep care for people left a lasting mark on me. Because of the way he loved others, I found myself reaching deeper, loving stronger, and caring more intentionally.

He frequently kept me informed about film opportunities, including the film Not Easily Broken, produced by DeVon Franklin.

During that season, I had the incredible opportunity to briefly speak into Taraji P. Henson's life. I'm certain many others had poured into her before and after me. But what struck me was how often I would see her afterward — in auditions, in projects, across the industry.

Everywhere I turned, there she was.

The lesson was not about proximity to fame. It was about obedience.

Obedience is crucial if you want to receive the fruit attached to your assignment. I believe one of my blessings manifested quickly after that final rehearsal — not because of who I met, but because I obeyed the prompting to speak when God nudged me.

Another divine connection.

Another reminder that it's never about status — it's about surrender.

I met Brother Fitz Houston through my cousin, who encouraged me to share my music with him. Two weeks later, Brother Fitz told me how God had distinctly instructed him regarding what to do for his TV show.

After wrestling with the decision concerning my music, and seeking God for clarity, he explained how the Lord told him why. From 5:30 a.m. until around 6:30 p.m. that evening, Fitz said he could not stop playing and listening to my music. Later, he understood why God instructed him to dedicate an entire TV show to me — not just to play my songs, but to feature my story.

To God be the glory — our arms are too short to box with God.

As I continued working as a security guard at Glendale Hospital, I later met a young gentleman whom I affectionately called my Little Bro Jeff. Jeffrey looked up to me not just as a coworker, but because we both loved God and His Word. We soon became close friends. Eventually, I was laid off from that position, and later realized it had not been a fair situation.

I returned to what I called my "fun job" — working security in the entertainment industry at events such as the Grammys, Emmys, BET Awards, and various theater venues.

During one particular event, I identified a stalker targeting certain celebrities. I confronted the individual before she could approach the main entrance to the courtyard. The situation grew intense, but I refused to let her pass. Eventually, an undercover officer intervened, realizing I had stepped into a serious situation.

Jeff became suicidal while I was ministering to another friend who was going through the same struggle. I was comforting her over a steak dinner when Jeff called, stating he was planning to end his life as well. I excused myself to the ladies' room so I could focus on what was happening with my little brother Jeff.

Through much exhortation and tough love, I convinced him not to take his life. As for my precious sister, she too decided not to end her life. Thank God.

When I returned home from the steakhouse, I called Jeff to check on him. He was completely at ease and had begun working on an old film project. At one time, that project had been accepted by the producer of the original Superman series. He wanted to add music and decided he wanted me to sing the songs he had tucked away.

My former husband, known as Jimi7Songs, had produced five bands, traveled the world multiple times, and played with Sammy Davis Jr. He would write a minimum of seven songs a day. While with him I met the pleasantly private and fun neighbors Ruth and Bobby Hendricks(The Drifters)

I enjoyed introducing Jimi7Songs to the Garage Band app, and we collaborated on several songs together. I helped copyright approximately thirty to forty of them. Unfortunately, he failed to complete the online verification process in time, and the copyrights were lost due to lack of response.

It was another lesson in stewardship, timing, and the weight of responsibility when creativity meets accountability.

Later on, I had the privilege of speaking with Al Green via his private cell phone. Al Green also impacted my Papi's life, contributing to my Papi's conversion to Jesus after more than thirty years in drug trafficking — the "Loved Fugitive" finally surrendering to the Lord.

I met other people of high caliber as well, but I simply received them as precious individuals. I was never star-struck — not then, not now. This was only a couple of months after serving as a security guard at the BET Awards, the Grammy Awards, the Emmy venues, and other major theaters.

One memorable experience involved assisting a Grammy choreographer and guitarist who had worked on the song "Fantasy Voyage." I helped him reshape six of his songs into spiritual and love songs for Jesus. Tragically, he later lost his life.

While married to my former husband, Jimi7Songs, he introduced me in 2011 to Larry and Luisa Dunn of Earth, Wind & Fire over the phone. As I was attempting to establish my first business, I spoke more extensively with Luisa regarding a particular situation. Little did I know that seven years later, I would have the opportunity to interview them in person.

Jumping ahead seven years — five of those years I spent homeless, experiencing Skid Row in downtown Los Angeles after separating from Jimi7Songs.

I believed I had a friend. But after signing a housing room contract and trying to help her, I was suddenly put out on the street. Her family came and went freely, yet I was the one forced to leave. Needless to say, things did not end well for my friend or her family.

I ended up homeless — even after assisting her with her TV shows in Pasadena, California.

Nevertheless, on one of those shows, I reconnected with Sister Luisa Dunn. It felt as though we had never missed a beat. Luisa smiled and said,

"Girl, let's do this!"

While in the green room, I was serving as the Director's Assistant (for my so-called friend), making sure the guest speakers were comfortable.

Brother Larry and Luisa Dunn had me constantly laughing. They were a complete delight. After that phenomenal taping, they signed their latest CD for me — a small but meaningful blessing during a difficult season.

While still homeless, I participated in a Skid Row Homeless Choir. One of the choir members took me in for a season, giving me temporary shelter and stability.

One day on the bus heading to church, a friendly voice asked,

"Where are you going with those gold shoes on?"

"To church," I replied.

"Wow, okay — which one?"

"Faithful Central Bible Church."

She exclaimed,

"Girl, that's my home church! Do you want to sit with me?"

"G-i-r-l, that's my home church!"

I had no clue that we would be sitting in the second row. I was accustomed to the back area, on the end, so I could dance freely unto my God and King. As time passed, I received a call from this newfound friend who needed more of my time and encouragement.

She began to confide in me as our friendship grew. One day she invited me to a concert. This wasn't just any concert — it was a celebration featuring The Four Tops and the last surviving member, none other than Abdul "Duke" Fakir.

My friend was the widow of MD George Roundtree of The Four Tops.

She took me into the dressing room and backstage. What a humbling experience — meeting her extended family and being welcomed so warmly.

Later, I volunteered to be part of a 500-member choir project. During a break, I befriended a precious sister. At first she was shy, but she quickly warmed up to me. As she began spending more time with me, I introduced her to the Skid Row Choir Urban Voice Project, which had become my home away from home for a season.

One day, she shared photos of her aunt — Aretha Franklin.

She spoke about how her aunt would often invite her places, sometimes even more than other family members. Over time, she came to realize that money wasn't everything. She felt compassion for her aunt and deeply respected her words of wisdom.

And in that moment, I realized something profound: God has a way of lifting you from the margins to the front row — not for prestige, but for purpose. From Skid Row to sitting among legends, from survival to significance, He was showing me that elevation is never accidental when it is orchestrated by His hand.

Then the King of Kings instructed me to take dominion through heavenly sound waves — to pierce the darkness. So I sang on.

I was yet amazed as I entered back into a love I had forgotten, my Messianic heritage and the Torah! Talking about such excellence to behold, I was divinely connected with Rabbi Amnon Shor, who was born in Israel to an orthodox Jewish family. His grandfather Zachariah was a Rabbi in the local synagogue. Rabbi Shor learned the Old Testament and the Jewish Law from early childhood. After his service in the Israeli Army, where he fought the Egyptian Army in the 1973 Yom Kippur War, he set out to see the world working for EL-AL Israel's Airlines , where he met his wife of 50 years Lynette. They have three children and seven grandchildren. He is a fifth generation Rabbi, from the Tribe of Judah! Loving the phenomenon teaching both in Hebrew and English and the love they so lavishly share.

Meanwhile, my cousin, who introduced me to yet another cousin, reassured me there would never be another like him. I still feel his warmth to this day, though he had an early graduation to Heaven — something he spoke of often and looked forward to. He never died alone. God never leaves nor forsakes those who call upon His name.

Listening to The Holy River, a song he wrote, I knew from his personal email that it was a revelation he had carried for some time. People can change for the better. They have the right to change. Though some remain fixed on old perceptions, God sees the transformation.

When you truly feel someone's heart, there is a depth of communication that cannot be explained. No one can tell you differently.

So I've placed "Cuz" in all my statements concerning him, because there will never be another Prince.

The promise from God between the four of us was that gorgeous rainbow stretched over his estate.

It was no different than the double rainbow I saw at my parents' graveside — one during my childhood and another in my adulthood.

That is the true meaning of a rainbow.

Straight from God, the Creator of the universe, to me personally — a divine reassurance that they are in Heaven.

"I have set My rainbow in the cloud, and it shall be a sign of the covenant between Me and the earth."

— Genesis 9:13

CHAPTER FOUR
FEEL ME — CHILDHOOD

Being a step ahead during my childhood — learning how to navigate rejection while anchoring myself in God's Word — became my quiet survival strategy.

Even as a little girl, I understood rejection.

I didn't just read about Moses, Joseph, David, and Jesus — I felt them. Rejected. Misunderstood. Set apart. Their stories weren't distant Bible accounts; they were mirrors. They became my companions in places no one else could reach.

I built a dream world — not to escape reality, but to survive it. Whenever I could connect what I was living to what I was reading, I felt less alone.

Though I was forced to attend church, something sacred happened there. It slowly stopped feeling forced. Especially during Vacation Bible School — that's where my heart softened.

That's where I found purpose.

I learned to serve early. I set up folding tables and metal chairs. I assembled props. I stayed late to sweep floors and carefully return supplies to their cubbyholes.

No one knew that each small task stitched something back together inside me.

Serving made me feel useful.

Useful made me feel seen.

Seen made me feel safe.

At the foster home, I longed for affirmation. For recognition. For someone to say, "You matter."

In the house of God, I began to sense that maybe... just maybe... I did.

The rewards were great and long-lasting, causing me to look for and depend on favor. The church family cheered me on far more than the foster family ever did—except for the oldest foster sibling, who was like my hero.

I could see that he gave his best in everything he did, yet he didn't receive the same recognition as the middle and youngest foster siblings. Learning early on from the underdog's perspective, I realized how much Ted never gave up. He always went the extra mile and always wore a smile.

But behind that smile, I could sense his heavy longing for real love and the pain in his heart. Because of him, I began to feel compassion for others.

I turned away from hatred and from poking pins into a doll during fits of rage against anyone who hurt me. I had been given a strange-looking doll that I thought was ugly—just like I had been told I was.

The youngest foster sibling often told me I was ugly and not liked. She would tell me to go play in my room where I "belonged" and to mind my own business. She was eleven years older than me, and whenever I received any kind of recognition, she would retaliate.

Whenever she could, she would grab me and dig her long, cat-like nails into my arm until blood came out. I was defiant and refused to cry.

We weren't allowed to tattle, so I couldn't report the abuse. I carried a lot of anger and rage during that time. Finally, I had enough. I began slapping her back hard enough to make her stop.

But the real battle wasn't between her and me. It was inside me.

Each time I fought back, I felt both powerful and ashamed. Powerful because I finally defended myself. Ashamed because I didn't want to become what was hurting me. I didn't want hardness to replace tenderness. I didn't want rage to define me.

So I learned something early: strength didn't always mean striking back. Sometimes strength meant surviving without losing my heart.

That lesson would follow me for the rest of my life.

Soon that ordeal faded from my life as she saw I was receiving attention from the oldest sibling, which caused her to withdraw from such vicious acts. Even the pin-poking doll ritual ceased, along with much of the hatred.

Eventually, I learned to turn rejection and pain into something else — almost like a game of survival. I decided I would try to live like the Bible characters I read about. In my make-believe world, I imagined I could be like Moses, Joseph, David — even Jesus — enduring rejection yet still chosen.

They fascinated me more than The Wizard of Oz, Cinderella, Mary Poppins, or even West Side Story.

After all, when that darkness crept over me like a heavy blanket and I lay paralyzed with fear, sensing death trying to overtake me, I discovered something powerful: just the thought of Jesus would disintegrate that presence. I recall that experience happening at least three times — always at night — when it felt like something was trying to take me out.

Fortunately, the "death angel" did not succeed.

But another hidden force remained — molestation.

The rule that I was not allowed to speak unless spoken to trapped me in silence. I could not share what was happening. That silence dulled my instincts — my caution, my fight-or-flight response — not only then, but in years to come.

My voice was suppressed.

My authority was denied.

And that unspoken powerlessness marked much of my childhood.

I was never abandoned.

I was being positioned.

CHAPTER 5

FEEL ME: TEENAGER

Jeremiah 29:11

"For I know the plans I have for you," declares the Lord,

"plans for peace and not for evil, to give you a future and a hope."

Jeremiah 33:3

"Call to Me, and I will answer you and tell you great and unsearchable things you do not know."

As I reflect back now, I realize something I did not understand then:

I do not have to remain a byproduct of generational pain.

I do not have to live in the shadow of the past —

of a parent's trauma,

of a relative's wounds,

of fear passed down silently like an inheritance.

I was in excruciating pain. A violent cramping twisted through my lower stomach, sharp and relentless, as if something inside me was about to burst. My head spun. I felt faint.

"Oh God... oh God..."

I couldn't hold it in any longer. I didn't dare scream. I could only groan through clenched teeth as the pain intensified. I took a deep breath, bracing myself for whatever was about to happen.

Then suddenly—

It was over.

A soft sound in the toilet. And just like that, the pain vanished.

The dizziness stopped. The nausea lifted. The pressure that had gripped my body disappeared instantly, as though it had never been there.

I stood there in shock, trembling, unsure of what had just taken place. I glanced down only briefly before quickly flushing. I didn't understand it. I didn't want to understand it.

All I knew was this: the terror was gone.

Slowly, I stood up, still shaken. I never told anyone. Not a word.

Weeks later, when my normal cycle returned, I felt an overwhelming sense of relief. Whatever I had feared... had passed.

But the fear itself — the trauma of thinking I was pregnant at thirteen — lingered far longer than the pain.

That moment altered something deep within me.

Even though nothing remained physically, the emotional imprint did. I began to equate purity with survival. Silence with safety. Shame with protection. If I stayed quiet... if I stayed "good"... if I stayed unseen... maybe nothing like that would ever threaten me again.

At thirteen, I carried a secret that felt heavier than my own body.

No one knew I had pleaded with God to "take the baby back to heaven." No one knew I had prepared myself to be rejected, exposed, thrown away. No one knew I believed my worth could be erased in a single mistake — even one forced upon me.

So I built walls.

I told myself I had to be pure. Not just morally — but invisibly pure. Untouchable. Unquestionable. I thought holiness meant never being vulnerable again.

But what I didn't understand then was this:

Purity is not the absence of pain.

Purity is not silence.

Purity is not shame.

Shame had tried to baptize me in secrecy.

But God never called me to carry what He had already covered.

I am not the byproduct of trauma.

I am not the echo of abuse.

I am not the shadow of generational pain.

I am redeemed.

What tried to break me did not define me.

What tried to shame me did not claim me.

What tried to silence me did not own my voice.

At thirteen, I thought I was losing everything.

But Heaven was preserving me.
The enemy tried to plant fear in my womb.
God planted destiny in my spirit.
And I stand today as living proof—
What was meant to destroy me
only deepened my dependence on God.
I am not bound by fear.
I am not governed by shame.
I am not controlled by the past.
I am growing through it.

CHAPTER 6

FEEL ME: ADULTHOOD

It was through that introduction that another connection quietly unfolded — one I did not fully recognize at first.

There was something familiar in his spirit.

Not just in appearance. Not in fame. Not in talent.

But in depth.

In the way he listened.

In the way he felt things.

In the way he carried both strength and sensitivity at the same time.

Some people enter your life loudly.

Others arrive like a whisper you don't understand until much later.

There was a warmth — a protective, almost brotherly presence — yet layered with an understanding that felt older than our meeting. Conversations were simple, yet beneath them ran something unspoken. A recognition.

I have learned that blood connects you by lineage.

But spirit connects you by design.

Even now, when I think of him, I do not think of platforms or stages.

I think of heart.

And I quietly say, "Cuz."

Because some connections are not meant to be explained.

They are meant to be honored.

And sometimes, God allows you to meet a reflection of your own journey — so you know you were never walking alone.

I LISTENED TO MY CUZIN

He said they couldn't hear between the lines...

I listened to my Cuzin.

He said they couldn't hear between the lines.

The lines of lust.

The lines of greed.

How can two walk together unless they agree?

Love matters — no devil can succeed.
There were choices I made for myself.
I wouldn't be controlled by anybody else.
Their hearts full of hate tried to paralyze —
Heaven captured me... captured me.
Soon they'll realize.
Who's gonna listen?
(Who, who, who...)
Who's gonna listen?
(Who, who, who...)
Cuzin, I listened.
Cuzin, I listened.
One look into Heaven — soon they would realize...
Heaven. Heaven. Heaven.
Before they could kill me.
Before they could drug me.
Heaven, Heaven, Heaven took me.
La La La La La La...
Now you can be free like me,
Yes — from this false galaxy.
Until it's your time to go —
Hey, no fear.
There's no fear.
I listened to my Cuzin.
I listened.
Heaven, Heaven, Heaven took me.
They only used me —
but Heaven took me.
"He that hath an ear, let him hear..."
— Revelation 2:7
I listened.
Not because I understood everything.

Not because I had proof.
But because something eternal whispered louder than the noise.
And when Heaven speaks between the lines...
survival becomes elevation.
That is how I learned to grow through it.
Evelyn Nelson © 2024
aka Silver Streak Lady ™

CONCLUSION

Singing in the Shadows concludes with a reflection on strength, survival, and the lessons learned through enduring life's trials. It highlights how I, through faith, music, and perseverance, overcame trauma and heartbreak. Despite facing immense losses, rejection, and abuse, I found healing in creativity and spiritual growth. Because I chose to be better and not bitter! The resilience shown throughout the journey hopefully inspires others to find their path to redemption, proving that even in the darkest shadows, hope can prevail.

Traumatized, Tattered and Torn(Lyrics)

You're walking through a deep and darkened valley

Can't see any light up ahead

Hold on to the Word God promised, and He'll do just what He said

Is there love, love, love Peace peace, peace Freedom

Freedom

Is there There's love There's peace

There's freedom, freedom, freedom

Is there anybody out there, out there that's been traumatized, tattered, and Torn

Ohhh is there anybody out there that's been

traumatized, tattered, and torn

DooDooDooDooDoo

FULL SCRIPTURE SECTION

The Word That Held Me

Psalm 23 (KJV)

The Lord is my shepherd; I shall not want.

He maketh me to lie down in green pastures: he leadeth me beside the still waters.

He restoreth my soul: he leadeth me in the paths of righteousness for his name's sake.

Yea, though I walk through the valley of the shadow of death, I will fear no evil: for thou art with me; thy rod and thy staff they comfort me.

Thou preparest a table before me in the presence of mine enemies: thou anointest my head with oil; my cup runneth over.

Surely goodness and mercy shall follow me all the days of my life: and I will dwell in the house of the Lord for ever.

Jeremiah 29:11 (KJV)

For I know the thoughts that I think toward you, saith the Lord, thoughts of peace, and not of evil, to give you an expected end.

Jeremiah 33:3 (KJV)

Call unto me, and I will answer thee, and show thee great and mighty things, which thou knowest not.

Psalm 27:10 (KJV)

When my father and my mother forsake me, then the Lord will take me up.

Revelation 2:7 (KJV)

He that hath an ear, let him hear what the Spirit saith unto the churches.

NOTES
TOO BLESSED TO BE STRESSED
I CHOOSE TO BE BETTER NOT BITTER
NO MORE TRAUMATIZED TATTERED & TORN

SUGGESTED READING

Holy Bible/The Complete Jewish Study Bible

Shout It From the Housetop by Pat Robinson

Harbinger I & II by Jonathan Cahn

Power Moves by Sarah Jakes Roberts

Undefeated by Shaunie Henderson

Take Me Back To The Truth by Annaniyah

Mickey & Debra C Galloway

Walk to Beautiful by Jimmy Wade

The Plant Paradox by Steven R Gundry. MD

The Rock, The Road and The Rabbi by Rabbi Sobel, Kathie Lee Gifford

The Jewish New Testament Narrated of Jonathan Settel/bonus

17 wonderful tracks narrated in Galilean Biblical Hebrew accent by Rabbi Amnon Shor

I Was Playing Checkers While God Was Playing Chess by James Bass

Charlie and the Magic Tree by Crystal Bass

PREFACE

Singing In the Shadows is the untold story of a woman born to a drug kingpin father, yet carrying the legacy of a renowned musician icon, cousin in her DNA. Despite being thrust into the foster care system, the silver thread of redemption never left her life, weaving through her pain and successes. With two murdered parents, domestic violence, and a near-death experience, her resilience shines. Join us as we unravel this journey, where music, divine connections, and unwavering faith guide her through life's roller coaster. Can we feel and hear God through her life —and in ours?

ABOUT THE BOOK

This musical allegory captures my struggles through childhood and adolescence. Despite the hardships of the foster care system, I emerged ready to roll with whatever happened. Then I felt my body lifting, l i f t i n g, lifting, and I was aware of this unexplained bright light as small as the tip of the head of a straight pin. I do remember saying, "God, "Wow, look at that light...!!!!!"

The next thing I knew, I was engulfed in this

indescribable heavenly pure white light, unsure how long I was there. When I came back into my body, the impact had me standing 4- 5 feet from the bed rather than in my bed on my back!

Silent, like gold refined in the fire, carrying the scent of Lilac and Lily of the Valley—a true Musical Garden. The name Silver Streak Lady represents redemption, fitting for a life where others entered to fill the void left by those taken violently from me. Though both parents were murdered, and I faced generational struggles and abuse, I found strength in a Source of Light and Life, carrying me through the unexpected. Despite rejections and setbacks, I resisted turning to alcohol or drugs, though my dependency on others nearly destroyed my destiny.

ABOUT THE AUTHOR

At age 39, my Papi Francisco Emmanuel Rodriquez graduated to Heaven causing my healed heart to still sing and encourage others to love and forgive. I enjoy eagles soaring, butterflies, double rainbows in the sky, and networking with people in the entertainment industry.

MUSIC

Recently, found out that my songs (8) were played in 72 countries. (FB 2023) CD BABY, MERCH, ASCAP, ISRC (International Standard Recording Code)

RADIO - My song "TRAUMATIZED TATTERED AND TORN was played on WOMEN of SUBSTANCE RADIO ...

SAG/AFTRA - GOOD TROUBLE, Very Coterie

Christmas via Disney WorldWide Services, Inc.

THEATERS - MY PAPI Story was shown in 50 THEATERS ACROSS Los Angeles County CA, presented by Homeward LA

(www.homewardla.org)

OCCUPATION

CAREGIVER - 50 years Personal & IHSS

Angels Agency

PERSONAL ASSISTANT - RUSS ROBINSON (My MUSICAL FATHER who trained me to sing major notes instead of minor notes, instructed me on how to be a PAGEANT

JUDGE for the Orlando Miss Teen pageant,

SECRETARY for INTERNATIONAL SONG

WRITERS GUILD(promotion fliers and PR

information), his PERSONAL SECRETARY(banking account update information)

SKILLS

LITERARY PUBLISHER of SILVER STREK LADY PRESS Books

Still Singing in the Shadows - eBook/Paperback/Hardcover Edition

LITERARY SONGWRITER

SONGWRITER. PRODUCER Songs

TRAUMATIZED TATTERED AND TORN, SILVER STREAK LADY, PROTECT THE CHILDREN, TELLIT LIKE IT IS, PROTECT THE

LOVED FUGITIVE, LIKE AN EAGLE, I CAN HEAR THE ANGELS SING, JAZZY

ANGELS SING, YOU GOT IT GOIN ON, FUN YOU GOT IT GOIN ON, FROM MY

HEART TO YOURS, LET'S CROSS THE BRIDGE TOGETHER, YOUNG LADY CHILD, BEYOND THE 70's, I LISTENED TO YOU COUZIN

ENGINEER PRODUCERS- John Dash Dixon Larry Treadwell, Roger Hunt

SINGERS - Sheryl Paige, Lenora Montgomery, CHAPLAIN Vondell Bradwell, Linda Armstrong, Kip Howard, Morilyn Crawford, Valencia Moore, Josiane Isidore, Jasmine Gonzales, Jessica Cikovic.

SPOKEN WORD - Giacomo Ben Ya'akov, Dwayne Winstead, Valencia Moore, Steven Moore, Stephan Moore, Brittany Harden, Tiffany Harden, Jennifer Thompson

SEAT FILLER for KELLY CLARKSON GAME SHOW

(CALIFORNIA"18 YEARS) SEAT FILLER for TEN different TV SHOWS (DEAL OR NO DEAL, JUDGE JOE BROWN, ALL OF US{WB}, THE WAR AT HOME{FOX},

'TIL DEATH{FOX},

AMERICA'S FUNNIEST VIDEOS{ABC},

ACCORDING TO JIM{ABC}, THE

CLASS{CBS}, THE NEW ADVENTURES OF OLD CHRISTINE{WB}, THE BIG BANG THEORY{CBS})

BET Awards

BACKGROUND ACTOR on ER as:

Environmental Services Personnel/Visitor Pedestrian Walking Wounded Deacon (child)

Stand-in/Sheena's mother (special guest child of Dare to Dream Org. this was her favorite evening program) Visitor

Medical Student/Visitor

Possible Double Stand in (Nurse Jeanne Boulet)

GOSPEL VIBES – Evelyn Nelson#56 (all my original music) VIMEO – Evelyn Nelson (all my original music)

MODELING it was a pleasure and fun: GALE JONES of DeBonius Creation-Fashion D` Passion (made me over 50 pieces of personal garments, modeled 5 pieces for his

bio & magazine article)

EXTRA PROFESSIONAL – Movie NOT EASILY BROKEN – with Taraji P. Henson & Morris Chestnut .

JESS ANDERSON Prod. Composite Co. MODELING (FLORIDA) Agency–modeling, RUNWAY for K-MART and

BACKGROUND PROFESSIONAL with CUBA

GOODING JR. on video 'IN THE SHADOWS'

.

CELEBRITY LOOK A LIKE– Alfre Woodard, Gloria Ruben, Gladys Knight, Tina Tuner, Ophra Winfrey and Whitney Houston (on the Body Guard movie), Kovac Benton

TRAINING I've received:

Russ Robinson– Frank Sinatra's Pianist 26 years, in over 120 films/ movies

Pro Staff Entertainment Security

Hey, I Saw Your Commercial-Commercials/TV

Training at Crossroads Security & Investigative Services

360* Degree Training Program for the Hollywood Industry

Free Access TV Producer

Program-Tampa Bay, FL

Community Network Free Access TV Producer Program-Rochester, NY

Beauty Charm Course - Caledonia, NY

SPECIAL SKILLS include:

CD Baby.com – CD SILVER STREAK LADY By Evelyn (Kelley) Nelson

WOMEN OF SUBSTANCE RADIO -—On LIVE365.COM (SUN. ET 3-5 or 9-11 AM/PT 12-2 or 6-8 AM)

TELL IT LIKE IT IS by SILVER STREAK LADY aka Evelyn Nelson MUSICXRAY.com Silver Streak Lady – Evelyn Nelson

WRITERS GUILD OF AMERICA, WEST, INC – TREATMENT Let Love Reign

SONGWRITER – Popular Pop, Neo Soul, Jazz, Contemporary Christian, R&B, Smooth, Velvet & Unique Duel Language Melodies

BILLBOARD SONGS

– Honorable Certificates of Songwriting Hits

TAXI – Member of The Worlds Leading Independent A&R Company matching your music w/films, commercials & movies

ASCAP - Member of the American Society of Composers, Author, and Publishers since 1988

AMERICAN SOCIETY OF POETS – Honorable Certificates from the US & London, Ambassador Choice Award & Editor Choice Award (2007)

ACKNOWLEDGEMENT

To my Father, Yahveh/God, Friend my Redeemer Deliverer, Savior and Lord, King of Kings, Yeshua/Jesus. To the Ruach Ha Kodesh/Spirit who teaches and guides me into all truth.

Rabbi Amnon Shor and Rebbetzin Lynette Lady Lynette - Bet Shalom, Fresno CA, are exemplary!

Mae Mae-Bernadette Diaz High Official Support Personal Assistant Heavenly Posted Ambassador Supernatural Knighted by the Trinity of Infinity My Spiritual Sister, Laughing Partner, Mae and Warrior Partner since 2004.

Co Pastor/Evangelist Mary J Tramel, my mom, Church of Hope That The Lord Has Made, Avon Park

CA Bishop William Baker - Executive Director, Producer,

Author and Motivational Speaker, WI

Prophet Navi Hughes - Voice of the Spirit Ministries, Orlando FL

Pastor James Baker - Church of Hope That The Lord has Made

Business Partner Cappie Stuff- CEO & Founder of RV for Homeless In just a few weeks, nearly 10 RVs and other essential items have been given away, with donations helping to support a waiting list of 500people. (https://rvforhomeless.com/)

She provides counseling and encouragement to those in need. Real Estate Experience: 10 years Intercessor

& Watchman for the Nations Bachelor's Degree in Theology TV Host on Free Access Station: "Parables of the End Times" Christian School Education: 11 years. She has ministered in churches, Bible schools, and colleges. Her long-term goal is to preach the Gospel worldwide.

CAPPIE STUFF CEO & Founder of RV for Homeless In just a few weeks, nearly 10 RVs and other essential items have been given away, with donations helping to support a waiting list of 500 people. She provides counseling and encouragement to those in need. Real Estate Experience: 10 years Intercessor & Watchman for the Nations Bachelor's Degree in

Theology TV Host on Free Access Station: "Parables of the End Times" Christian School Education: 11 years. She has ministered in churches, Bible schools, and colleges. Her long-term goal is to preach the Gospel worldwide.

www.ingramcontent.com/pod-product-compliance
Lightning Source LLC
LaVergne TN
LVHW091813110826
845146LV00006B/1122

* 9 7 9 8 9 9 2 3 2 5 3 4 8 *